T0198408

A WISH IN THE NITE

CAL

To order additional copies of this book, contact:
Xlibris
844-714-8691
www.Xlibris.com
Orders@Xlibris.com

ISBN: Softcover   978-1-6641-6252-5
         EBook   978-1-6641-6251-8

Print information available on the last page

Rev. date: 03/09/2021

A WISH IN THE NITE

Written by RCM

Introduced by CAL

Cover artist Rachael Plaquet

I want a friend and a confidant
I want a partner and an advisor

I want someone who would walk
Through life beside me
Sometimes ahead, but never behind me!!

I want someone who could possess my soul
Someone that would haunt my dreams

And could firmly but warmly hold
my heart in her hands

I want a lover
Both spiritually and physically

I want a woman who knows the difference
Between having sex and making love

Making love without having sex
Can be so much more intimate
So much more fulfilling
I want someone with an opinion

I want a woman who could take a little flack
When she deserved it
One that could put me in my place
When I needed it
But never in the presence of others

I want someone who would smile as she slept
When I roll over in the night to kiss her
shoulder and tell her that I love her

I want someone who would cry for me
and not just because of me

I want a strong independent woman
Who doesn't need me but wants me

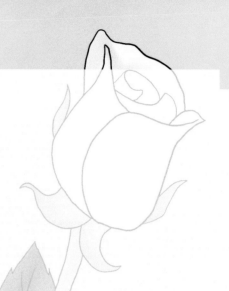

I want a woman that would allow me
To take care of her
And let me hold her
Just because I want to

I want someone who would have a
Glass of wine with me as we
walked hand in hand
Together on the beach
And watched the sunset
One who would stay up late with me
To gaze at the stars after mid night
They're brighter then

I want a woman who would
Appreciate the smaller things in life
Like the gift of some favourite candy
Or a blue rose
Delivered on a rainy afternoon

I want a woman who would share with me
Her greatest joys and triumphs
Her deepest sorrows and disappointments
One that would listen to mine
And not judge me because of them

I want a woman who would love me
as much as I might love her
I would love her with every fiber of my being!
I want someone who would hold me when I die....

Printed in the United States
by Baker & Taylor Publisher Services